sisters

Published by Willow Creek Press, Inc.
P.O. Box 147, Minocqua, Wisconsin 54548

Photo Credits:

p4 © Yva Momatiuk & John Eastcott/Minden Pictures; p6 © Stefan Meyers/Ardea.com;
p9 © Ron Kimball/KimballStock; p10 © Klein-Hubert/KimballStock; p14 © Juniors Bildarchiv/age fotostock;
p17 © Gouichi Wada/Nature Production/Minden Pictures; p18 © Dani Carlo/Prisma/age fotostock;
p20 © John Lund/KimballStock; p23 © Frank Parker/age fotostock; p24 © Jean Michel Labat/Ardea.com;
p27 © Konrad Wothe/Minden Pictures; p28 © John Daniels/Ardea.com; p31 © Ferrero-Labat/Ardea.com;
p34 © Daniel J. Cox/Natural Exposures; p37 © Klein-Hubert/KimballStock;
p41 © Mark J. Barrett/KimballStock; p42 © Lisa & Mike Husar/www.TeamHusar.com;
p45 © Joe & Mary Ann McDonald/KimballStock; p46 © Augusto Stanzani/Ardea.com;
p49 © Flirt/SuperStock; p50 © Robert Winslow/KimballStock;
p53 © Lisa & Mike Husar/www.TeamHusar.com; p54 © Joe & Mary Ann McDonald/KimballStock;
p57 © Mike Osmond/Ardea.com; p58 © Klein-Hubert/KimballStock;
p61 © Ron Kimball/KimballStock; p62 © Robert Winslow / KimballStock;
p65 © Daniel J. Cox/Natural Exposures; p66 © John Daniels/KimballStock;
p69 © Klein-Hubert/KimballStock; p70 © Klein-Hubert/KimballStock;
p72 © Richard Stacks/KimballStock; p75 © Robert Winslow/KimballStock;
p76 © Jan Vermeer/Foto Natura/Minden Pictures; p79 © Sylvain Cordier/peterarnold.com;
p80 © John Cancalosi/Ardea.com; p83 © Sabine Stuewer/KimballStock;
p84 © Lisa & Mike Husar/www.TeamHusar.com; p87 © Jagdeep Rajput/Ardea.com;
p88 © Daniel J. Cox/KimballStock; p91 © Gary Randall/KimballStock;
p92 © Thomas Dressler/age fotostock; p95 © P. Narayan/age fotostock

Design: Donnie Rubo
Printed in Canada

Sisters

A Force To Be Reckoned With

Bonnie Louise Kuchler

WILLOW CREEK PRESS®

For Vada and Eva

Table of Contents

Four Arms, Four Legs, One Heart—
Sharing & Bonding

My sisters are as constant and familiar
as fixed stars in the night sky.
They are my geography.

—Debra Ginsberg, American author

The history that sisters have shared
is tucked away in their own magic lamp,
waiting to be conjured up at the rub of a single word:
Christmas... chores... chickenpox...
pets... punishments... parents...
bathroom... boyfriends... borrowing...
secrets... and home.

—Bonnie Louise Kuchler

I shared space with her—
both mental and physical—
and wished only that she'd stay
put on her side of the bed.

—Patricia Foster, American author

Sisterhood is not just
about sharing genes.
It's about sharing jeans.

—Natalie Evans (quoted in *Sisterhood*)

Most things, most people are
frills; they are trimming.
Sisters are part of your fabric.

—Bonnie Louise Kuchler

I carry her in my mind as the real one,
the original, the *aleph* to my *beth*,
the word to which I am the rhyme.

—Bonnie Friedman, American author

I substituted... her face for any face described.
Whatever the author's intentions,
the heroine was my sister.

—Mavis Gallant (b. 1922), Canadian author

She's Taller, My Nose Is Smaller— Comparing & Competing

Sisters can't help themselves.
From birth to the grave
and from head to toe
they will compare
who is cuter, who is skinnier,
who is smarter;
whose children are cuter, skinnier, smarter;
whose grandchildren are
cuter, skinnier, smarter;
and who has more wrinkles.

—Bonnie Louise Kuchler

A sister's mere existence provides a woman
with a constant source of comparison...
she is a walking yardstick.

—Vikki Stark, American author, family therapist, educator

You can't help but rub each other when you're forming who you are.

—Joanna Kerns (quoted in *Sisters Are Like Sunshine*)

I suppose there are sisters
who don't compete.
I have never met one.

—Lisa Grunwald, American author

Sisters understand...
why the skirt you adored in the
Hip-Hop Chicks Boutique
suddenly looks totally tacky, ugly,
and uncool the minute your
sister flicks a glance
over it and says, "Why'd
you buy *that* thing?"

—Lorraine Bodger, American author

Approval from a sister
weighs much heavier
than from a friend.

—Diane Werts, American author

I envy her with all my heart, for she is
the side of me that God left out.

—Lillian Gish (1893-1993), American actress, about her sister Dorothy

Time Travel—
Reminiscing & Remembering

Sisters were time traveling long
before sci-fi was born.
When grown sisters come together,
they step through a portal
and emerge as little girls.

—Bonnie Louise Kuchler

Sisters remember things you would rather forget. In graphic detail... With proof.

—Marion C. Garretty (quoted in *The Love Between Sisters*)

You keep your past by having sisters.
As you get older, they're the only ones who
don't get bored if you talk about your memories.

—Deborah Moggach, British novelist

Reminiscing with your sister is like pressing rewind in a world stuck on fast forward.

—Bonnie Louise Kuchler

I wish that I could escape,
were it only for a quarter of an hour,
to breathe that air in which we
lived for many years.

—Edma Pontillon (1839-1921), in a letter to her sister, artist Berthe Morisot

A pleasure is full grown only
when it is remembered.

—C. S. Lewis (1898-1963), Irish author

Quibbling by Siblings—Quarreling & Squabbling

The kettle of sibling emotions bubbles
beneath the surface, restless to boil over.

—Bonnie Louise Kuchler

Never let an angry sister
comb your hair.

—Patricia McCann, American radio personality

If we are the younger, we may envy the older.
If we are the older, we may feel that the younger
is always being indulged.
In other words, no matter what position
we hold in family order of birth, we can prove
beyond a doubt that we're being gypped.

—Judith Viorst, American author and poet

We were born ten minutes apart...
She always said she was the real baby,
and I was a kind of backup.

—Adair Lara, American author, columnist, teacher

Why is it so hard to act like an
adult around your sister?...
Everything you do seems to
be equal parts habit,
compulsion, and voodoo forces
beyond your control.

—Lesley Dormen, American author

Sisterhood is a lifelong dance.
There is holding and lifting,
leading and following,
kicking and spinning,
and always ups and downs.

—Bonnie Louise Kuchler

X-ray Vision with Extrasensory Perception— Knowing & Understanding

A sister sees straight through your mask...
She knows if you're telling the truth.
She knows if you're *mostly* telling the truth.
She sees your hidden motives.
She sees *whatever* it is you're hiding.
And she knows when you're hurting,
because she sees all the
way into your heart.

—Bonnie Louise Kuchler

You can kid the world, but not your sister.

—Charlotte Gray, British-born Canadian author and historian

Sisters don't need careful explanations.
They don't even need full sentences.

—Pamela Dugdale, writer (quoted in *Sisters!*)

No one else knows what I mean so exquisitely,
painfully well; no one else knows
so exactly what to say, to fix me.

—Joan Frank, American author

We let down our guard for our siblings day after day,
year after year, without thinking about it much.
We share with them real life.
We've seen them naked,
in every imaginable sense of the word.

—Nick Kelsh, American author and photographer &
Anna Quindlen, American author and columnist

No one can understand
you like your sister.
She's comprised of all the
same parts you are.

—Claudine Gandolfi, author

There's something beautiful about finding
one's innermost thoughts in another.

—Olive Schreiner (1855-1920), South African author, anti-war campaigner

She's My Sister—
Protecting & Defending

Sisters are bodyguards,
joined at the hip.
They are also heartguards,
separated enough to see clearly
when the other is too close to focus.

—Bonnie Louise Kuchler

The mildest, drowsiest sister has been known to turn tiger if her sibling is in trouble.

—Clara Ortega (quoted in *The Love Between Sisters*)

I have always loved my sister's voice.
...a greening thing, an enemy of
storm and dark and winter.

—Pat Conroy, American author

I know that whatever the disaster
I blunder into, you will rescue me.
Pausing only to tell me what
an idiot I've been.

—Pam Brown, Australian poet and author

No matter what life throws at you,
she'll help you catch as
much as she can.

—Kelly Pullen (quoted in *Sisterhood*)

Sisters together are a force
to be reckoned with.

—Karen Brown, American writer

Sisters Are All from Venus— Comforting & Loving

Sisters know instinctively that love is a verb.
When a sister says "I love you," she's not saying
she feels warm and fuzzy. She's telling you...
If you cry, I will cry too;
I will keep your darkest and most precious secrets;
If you call, I will answer—even at 2 a.m.;
If you're in the hospital, I will hop on
a plane to hold your hand;
If you're in a hard place, I will lend you money;
If you need a kidney, you can have one of mine;
And if the worst happens, I will raise your children.

—Bonnie Louise Kuchler

Sisterhood is powerful.
Like volcanoes.
Like earthquakes.
Like tornadoes.
Like love.

—Bonnie Louise Kuchler

The way to love someone is
to lightly run your finger
over that person's soul
until you find a crack,
and then gently pour your
love into that crack.

—Keith Miller, American author and inspirational speaker

My sister is truly one of the comforts of my life—a little like putting tired, pinched feet into warm, soft slippers.

—Ellyn Sanna, author

I want to be where she is.
It is not a very conscious feeling—
just a vague discontent with
the places she is not...
I get up and follow her when
she moves from one room to another
as one might unconsciously follow
a moving patch of sunlight in a room.

—Anne Morrow Lindbergh (1906-2001), married
to aviation pioneer Charles A. Lindbergh, Jr.

A sister is
a coach, a cheerleader, a teammate and a rival—
sometimes all in one day.
She blazes the trail;
she hides in your shadow.
She's an audience of one,
and a dazzling star.
Sometimes she's a conscience,
sometimes she's a cohort,
but always, she's a soft place to land.

—Bonnie Louise Kuchler

The End